FINDING YOUR PEACE

THE MAGIC OF LIVING HERE AND NOW

FIVE DECADES OF EXPLORING INNER SPACE

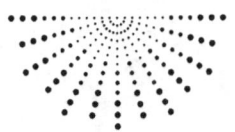

BRIAN HESTON

Meditation, Gratitude and Happiness, a 51 year incredible journey

Dedicated to Prem Rawat
Who taught me life is magical
And to
Eugene & Doris Heston
Who gave me love, trust and never held me back,
Susan Heston who encouraged creativity,
And Nitza Ohana who appreciated me and my creativity

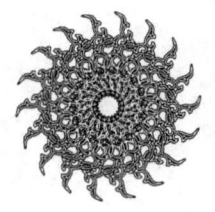

COPYRIGHT

FOREWORD

Be here now.

If you are anywhere near my age- you know that's a thing...

So many people have told me to "live in the "NOW." I could scream. You can't change the past... HOW do I live in the now? What is the now? Will someone tell me?

I wasn't sure what now was: in between loads of laundry... the kids crying... my endless miserable legal battle with a sociopathic ex-husband?

Then I met Brian.

Brian didn't tell me anything I didn't know before. He seemed to have an unusual ability to cut through the *bad neighborhoods* and arrive in fun, interesting places.

I instantly recognized that Brian was just a rare individual who had never been ensnared in anyone else's expectations and had a lot figured out.

Brian is balanced and centered. It was clear that he was

choosing to stay balanced. At 6' and barely 165 lbs, he could easily topple over in a gust of wind.

How does he stay rooted?

Brian credits his parents Gene and Doris, who I never met, and his teacher Prem Rawat with providing some very useful techniques for re-balancing when things go wobbly.

I imagine Brian's parents and his childhood home life as pretty idyllic. Brian was a late-life gift-baby, very much anticipated and adored by an extended family, with parents, an older sister, and grandparents all living under one roof. By all accounts, he was an ordinary sweet, kind gentle child. I argue that Brian already had everything he needed to live

Prem is not a faith healer or a religious leader. He could have been. You could argue that Prem Rawat was *destined* to be a spiritual leader or even a cult figure. He chose to stay in his lane. He enjoys what he does. His joy is infectious. Prem wanted to talk to people, share his message of peace, and bring peace to an unpeaceful world. He's doing just that for over 61 years.

I met Brian when he was 63 years old. He instantly struck me as someone who ALWAYS followed his heart. He liked planes, so he learned to fly one. He liked to make things, so he made things out of wood. He enjoyed photography and technology, so he figured out how to work that into a career.

Now, Brian is just beginning his 70th year. He has experienced a lot. He's known some personal tragedy and come through it whole.

There was a moment when Brian appeared in my life, and I had a choice: trust my heart... or move on.

Brian was non-critical, loving and very non-judgmental. He is not naturally given to public speaking, but he does have a lot to say.

All he did was discourage me from falling into my habitual practice of fear... anxiety, lack of clarity.

I had been *practicing* fear, anger, and anxiety, and I had become very good at it. I was attached to my misery because I had identified with it for so long. I refer to myself as a *deep-well of endless misery!* I often asked Brian why he wanted to stick around. I think on some level, Brian is a healer who found a good patient. I was a good project. He could practice what he learned from his charmed life on me. I was willing to change course, a bit reluctantly.

I've made progress. I had some ballast to begin with and luckily I had not lost all faith in my humanity.

I am grateful to Brian, to his parents, to Susan and to Prem:

I don't know how or why he does it but Brian is a soothing, calming presence and he wanted to tell his story:

If this were my book, I would dedicate it to Brian.

This is Brian's story in his own words.

Nitza Ohana

INTRODUCTION

Please allow me to introduce myself; my name is Brian Keith Heston. I was born in November 1953 in Cleveland, Ohio, and have lived a magical life. Just when you think it can't get any better than this….. it does.

The purpose of this book is to share with the reader the things I most credit for making my life so magical and how you might also live a charmed life full of joy, peace, and fulfillment. I ask that you read with an open mind and an open heart. I don't ask you to accept anything that does not already resonate as true within yourself.

This is both a story of a life and a guide to living well, no matter your circumstances.

What are you looking for in life? Peace of mind like you get sitting on a mountaintop or next to a mountain stream? Relief from the stress of your job? Finding your soulmate?

That and more can be found in exploring inner space.

Or at least if it won't find a soulmate for you, it will give you clarity on what that is and will put you in the right place at the right time to find them. As a human being, you are already complete. The feeling that something is missing (i.e., soulmate) may be because you do not recognize you are already complete.

"What you are looking for is inside of you" - *Prem Rawat*

I am a wealthy man of modest means. That is, financially, I am comfortable, not wealthy compared to many, but not enduring much austerity either (I have known austerity).

In matters <u>not</u> of this world, I hit the jackpot, and that's part of the motivation to write this book. I have something to say, and if, in saying it, one person hits their own jackpot and was helped by the words herein, then this book has value.

Do not be a prisoner of your thoughts, emotions and concepts
We can easily make the mistake of thinking that is all we are.

1

CHOICE

ANXIETY , FEAR, AND ANGER OR PEACE, LOVE AND JOY

*P*eace, joy, clarity, rage, sadness, and fear are choices. Recognize it.

Anyone who has felt lost in confusion can tell you that choice does not always seem possible.

To feel gratitude can seem elusive when you're caught up in dark feelings. It can feel like you are trapped. Choose gratitude over feeling blue. How? First, turn your attention to your breath, feel it come into you and go out, and recognize the rhythm of life and the value of breath. Now, consider what you did to earn that breath. Nothing? Is it a gift? Right? A priceless gift that can't be bought. Ask a rich man on his deathbed what he'd pay for another breath. If you are alive, you have a priceless gift.

Breath … is one thing we all have in common that you can easily take for granted. It is probably the most under-appreciated and the most valuable thing we have. It facilitates life; it connects us to each other, to the plants and animals, earth and sky. It's invaluable because it can't be bought but is given as a gift.

The air that you breathe is, science tells us, made up of billions of atoms. I've read that: there are more atoms in a human body than stars in the entire universe—some of those atoms we have in common. According to science, our bodies contain atoms breathed by everyone who has ever lived. So we are all connected in ways I never really thought much about. Pretty amazing when you consider the implications. I'm breathing some of the same atoms as you and some of the same atoms as cavemen, Ben Franklin and Leonardo. A bit mind-boggling, to be sure.

Each of us is unique. There has never been anyone like you, nor will there be again. It took 13 billion years of evolution to create a human being that is you.

Indeed, many of us find excuses to wallow in misery, "I can't because [fill in the blank]" First, you must take responsibility for your past choices and recognize them as your choice, good or bad. It's okay; you are a human being. Mistakes are alright. They may have consequences, but it's okay, so forgive yourself.

Never feel like a victim. You chose your situation, good or bad. If it is really bad a part of me wants to blame my dilemma on the other instead of recognizing my choice. It often seems easier to blame someone else than to accept responsibility. But, if I want to free myself, I must take responsibility for my choices.

The voice in your head is not always pleasant to you. It causes suffering and picks on you. You must also be willing to leave your familiar anxieties behind. If you've been practicing fear, anger, and anxiety for any time, you may have become very good at it. You can become attached to your misery because you have identified with it for so long that you may even think that's who you are. You are *not* a *deep well of misery,* let me assure you. You are so much greater than that. Your thoughts of suffering may confuse your very understanding of yourself. Who am I? What am I?

"KNOW THYSELF" - *Socrates.*

"Watch out now,
    Take care, beware now,
    of thoughts that linger
    Winding up inside your head
    The hopelessness around you
    In the dead of night
    Beware of sadness
    It can hit you
    It can hurt you
    Make you sore, and what is more
    That is not what you are here for...." George Harrison.

THE LACK of recognition of your inner Self creates much of the world's suffering. Inner Self? What do I mean by

Inner Self? Another word for it is *essence*. Rabbi Simon Jacobson calls it the *soul*; he would say suffering is the soul's plea for attention, for recognition. If the body needs attention, it lets you know with thirst, hunger, or maybe a muscle ache. If the soul is neglected, it lets you know, too, with sadness, confusion, perhaps even fear, anxiety, or anger.

Rabbi Jacobson went on to say when he meets someone, he frequently asks, "Who are you?" The person often responds by offering a business card. "This is what you do, not who you are. Who are you?" The person usually replies that they are defined by what they do, that is, who they are. The Rabbi says that is the inverse of what it should be; what the person does should be defined by who they are if they know who they are. They look at themselves from the outside looking in rather than from within looking out. There is a song within each of us, a unique piece of music that is a part of your Soul. If we would all know our song and express it as those around us also express it: there would be a symphony in which each voice was indispensable and together created the most beautiful of harmonies.

"Alas to those that die with their song still inside them."
  - Oliver Wendell Holmes

Do not get confused by the voice in your head. You are something much greater than the chatterbox between your ears. There are practical techniques for experiencing *Knowledge of the Self*, not belief, faith, or reading about it.

Know by your own experience that you contain a treasure of being alive and have the capacity to experience that infinite universal one. Not belief or simply reading about, but if you let go and dive in, there is no bottom, no top, no sides to the seat of the soul deep within the stillness. There is nothing to fear about that experience. It is both familiar and comforting. After all, where did you come from?

The running commentary in your head keeps you thinking about things that either happened in the past or have not even happened. Anger is an unpleasant feeling we are all familiar with. It is the result of something in the past, a perceived injustice that we bang up against repeatedly. It can chew you up. Fear is about the future - this might happen, that could happen. What if? Some fear makes sense; if someone points a gun at you, fear is a normal reaction. I'm not saying all fear is always wrong, sometimes it can help save you from harm, but you should not let it carry you away. Listen to your heart, and make it the captain of your ship.

If confronted with a frightening situation, I'd like to think I'd follow my breath to the connection with my heart and let my heart choose what action, if any, was warranted.

Anger and fear are rooted in the past and the future. In other words, they don't exist; are they our inner Self calling for attention? They keep you from enjoying the peace and fulfillment that is Now. Or, is it that since we were distracted away from fulfillment, it is a reminder to come back to the place of fulfillment, to Now? Whether you see it as a cry for attention from a neglected part of yourself depends on your perception. If you have been lost for a long time, you may not see it as a cry for attention from the Soul or Self.

The *True Self* is also sometimes called the *Atman*: Let us explore;

Ātman (Hinduism) - Wikipedia
   https://en.wikipedia.org › wiki › Ātman_(Hinduism)

Ātman is a Sanskrit word that **refers to the (universal) Self or self-existent essence of individuals,** as distinct from ego (Ahamkara), mind (Citta) and ...

Jul 16, 2020 — Atman is a Sanskrit word, defined in simple terms as **an individual's inner self, spirit or soul**. The concept of Atman as the true self is ...

— HTTPS://WWW.YOGAPEDIA.COM/
DEFINITION/5245/ATMAN

IT CAN SEEM VERY difficult to let go of fear and anger, past and future. First, realize you are choosing anger and anxiety, and you have a choice. Choose instead not to give it the power to keep you from enjoying your life. It is, after all, your life. If you want to enjoy it, stop giving away your control. If you need to forgive someone for making you angry, do so; after all, we are all human beings. Human beings make mistakes. I am not suggesting that there is no place for anger sometimes to counter bad behavior. It helps to show some anger but remain in control. Sometimes my stepson would behave poorly, and to let him know it was not alright, I'd have to be or pretend to be angry. I think we all know the feeling of anger that eats at you and anger that is used to show displeasure with bad behavior and then let go of it.

Is there a better choice in moments of anger, fear, and hate?

To be conscious of, and follow the heart. I have lived most of my life by that principle. I've yet to regret any of those choices.

To know the stillness within, to exist at the moment called NOW, requires you to quiet the voice in your head that is primarily busy judging or fearing or being pissed off because to listen to it is not to BE. Let it chatter, but focus your attention elsewhere. When I AM a human BEING, each breath is like a caress of the creator to the created—always anchoring me in the now.

The trick to letting go is quite simple once you decide to let go. Replace your judgment or fear with the recognition that it is not real and is keeping you from experiencing the joy that is your birthright; pay attention to your breath and realize this breath is giving me life, feel gratitude for the gift of life, don't try to still your mind instead let it observe your breath. It will become gradually still, and you'll be experiencing the joy of knowing you are alive at that moment; if you can go deep enough to experience the life energy behind your breath, it is beautiful. At first, you may only achieve a few moments of stillness before your mind gets distracted. Just bring your attention back to your breath, and the voice in your head will be quiet.

"Energy can neither be created nor destroyed" - Albert Einstein.

There are emotional storms in every life, but if you are deeply anchored, the branches may bend in that storm, but they will not break. Emotions come and are experienced fully and acknowledged, but they do not run the show. Being rooted within, you can experience grief, loss, and upheaval without uprooting.

After all, birth and death are two sides of the same coin. Everyone alive was born and will die. That is a certainty. It's what goes on between birth and death that is important. Whether we spend all of our time focusing on the world without ever acknowledging the world within or recognizing the beauty within, that is glimpsed by most but embraced only by those who have learned to love immersion in peace, for that still place is where love originates. Love of the creator for the created, the infinite for the finite. There are many forms of love and expressions of love, but as I have heard many times in India, "god is love, and...love is god" are simple words but meaningful. Love connects all of creation, and there is no greater love than the creator's love for the created, and the most fulfilling experience of the created is to know that love. To be immersed in that experience. Human beings can Know that fulfillment and can experience that love.

I don't want this book to be another book of esoteric theories to entertain the mind; what I am talking about can only be known by the heart. It must be experienced and felt. It can not be known by thought alone.

Some think they need to immerse themselves in the wilderness, in nature, to return to that state of peace. Indeed nature, at its best, exemplifies calm, still peacefulness. I love to be in nature as much as anyone, but I recognize the need to find the quiet; still serenity inside of me lest the noise of the chattering monkey mind follows me into that sanctuary.

So I hope that I have established this writer's perspective and will begin my story or stories. The day you are born, your story begins, and each day you get to write another page until the day you die, and the book closes. What story will you write? I have lived so many stories. They all intersect, connect and fit into a lifetime. I could begin at the beginning and spin and weave all these stories together, But I may not wish to devote that much of my time to the telling when new stories are being made even now.

However long or short your life may be, know that your days are numbered, and only you can choose how to spend them. When they are spent, that's it; you can't get any more. So, choose wisely how you will spend yours.

"All know the drop merges with the ocean; few understand the ocean also merges with the drop" - Kabir.

"You are the drop. There's an ocean in this drop. I can put you in touch with the ocean in the drop," Prem Rawat.

* * *

2
SEEKER

I remember thinking something was wrong with the adult world as a child. My parents, great-aunts, and grandmother were very loving, and I had an ideal childhood in many ways. It just seemed like adults had forgotten how to have fun. Was that my destiny? I hoped not. At 14, my Dad took me to a father/son banquet at church. I remember Cleveland Browns wide receiver Paul Warfield was the speaker. I don't remember what he said though it struck me profoundly. I stayed up most of the night jotting down notes as I experienced one Aha! Moment after another. I was experiencing Clarity, and it so excited me that I was set on a path to find my way back there. When I was 16 and 17, my seeking led me to Hatha Yoga, Kundalini Yoga, Zazen, and psychedelics like Mescaline, Magic Mushrooms, and LSD. New research has shown the benefits of these drugs. Though I don't advocate their use, they may take you to that Clarity that is found in bliss, but they are only temporary. Depending on the environment they are taken in, they can also cause harm. If you are thirsty, you can skip to the chapter 14 on Resources and find the link to Peace Education And Knowledge. Otherwise, I promise if you are not in a hurry, read on, and our path will take us there.

When I was 17, my friend, David, told me about his cousin, Nelson, who lived in a teepee in Breckenridge, Colorado, before it became the ski resort it is today. It was still basically a ghost town. Nelson told of a 13 yr old Indian boy, a satguru who could look you up and down, and if your aura showed you had good karma, he could open your third eye with a touch. I had just finished reading a book called *The Third Eye* by T. Lobsang Rampa, so I was primed. Now this story turned out to be not entirely accurate, but there was a 13 yr old Indian boy who proclaimed, "what you are searching for is inside you, and I can show it to you." Nelson went to India with the 13 yr old Indian boy, who was known as Satguru Maharaj Ji or Guru Maharaji (given name Prem Rawat). When Nelson returned from India, he stopped in Cleveland, and he and his friend, Lucky, who got his name while serving as a tunnel rat in Vietnam, both had much to say about Guru Maharaji and the Knowledge he was offering. It was December 1971; we found out that one of Guru Maharaji's mahatmas, who were empowered to give his Knowledge (Knowledge throughout this book, when capitalized, refers to specific techniques for meditation), would be in Chicago in January. So we traveled to Chicago and saw this bald brown man in a saffron robe and a 1000-watt smile. There were 5 or 6 of us from Cleveland. The mahatma gave a talk one night to maybe 100- 200 people and invited anyone interested in receiving the Knowledge to return the next day. We returned the following day and found about 20 people there to ask for Knowledge. Some asked questions, but every time I looked at that 1000-watt smile, it seemed my questions were answered before I could raise my hand. So Mahatma Ji asked each of us if we understood the preciousness of what was being given and if we agreed to practice. When it was my turn, I answered yes and was invited to join the Knowledge session. So on January the twelfth nineteen hundred and seventy-two, I received the Knowledge of Self. I was, to put it mildly, blown away. I was back to that experience I had as a 14 yr old plus been shown four techniques to have that experience anytime! I could dive as deep into it as I wanted. No drugs needed, no years of spinal flexes, and breath of fire. I was elated and wanted to tell everyone I knew about this Knowledge. Let me offer my profound apologies now to anyone I may have encountered then and turned off seeking this experience for themself by my enthusiasm.

As I practiced the techniques known as Knowledge, I found myself more centered, grounded, and rooted in a calm and peaceful place at a minimum and, at times, completely blissed out.

As the teenage guru matured, he recognized that all the Indian trapping around him was limiting. Though many people in the early 70s were attracted to eastern thought and all its trappings, many were not. So, Satguru

Shri Sant Ji Maharaj, Guru Maharaji, became Prem Rawat. I once heard Prem say he'd answer "Hey You" if he dropped his wallet.

* * *

Seeker

3

FOUND IT!

A LIFETIMES JOURNEY

*S*earching for self-knowledge is a lot like looking for your glasses when they're on top of your head, or your phone when it's in a pocket. It's already within you.

A story Prem or a Mahatma told me goes like this: Once upon a time, there was a student and a master. The student, we'll call Ahmed.

Ahmed had many worldly desires and thought if he could fulfill many of them, he would find peace. He went to the master and begged for a Genie to fulfill his desires. The master told him a Genie is far too dangerous. "You know Genies come with big curved swords, and they must be kept busy all the time, or they will take their sword and cut off your head." Ahmed thought about it and thought, I have so many desires to be fulfilled - no problem. So he begged his master to give him a Genie until finally, the master reluctantly agreed. He went home and opened the door and there was the genie, curved vast sword already in his hands, saying, "What is your wish, master" and hefting the sword. Ahmed said, "Genie, bring me a four-course meal of chicken, rice, vegetables, and delights." The genie replies, "Yes, master, your wish is my command," and poof disappears. A moment later reappears, and there is the most sumptuous meal in front of the man". The man is salivating at the smell and sight of this fantastic meal, and just as he is about to take the first bite, the genie says, "What is your wish master" hefting the sword again. The man thinks of another desire to be fulfilled, and the genie exceeds expectations, but again just as he is about to enjoy it, he hears, "What is your wish, master," and there stood the genie hefting the sword. This continued until Ahmed was having trouble thinking of new things for the genie, so he went running back to his master and begged him to take the genie back, but the master told him, " I cannot. I warned you, but you foolishly ignored me. Now you must live or die with the consequences " Ahmed was beside himself. Please, master, tell me what to do; I'll do anything you ask. Please save me from the genie. The master said to him tell your genie you want him to go out into the middle of the desert and construct a pole 20 feet tall. Then, he is to climb to the top of that pole, and when he reaches the top, he must descend to the bottom, rise again to the top, and repeat that process until you summon him.

Isn't the mind a bit like the genie? And isn't breath a little like the pillar in the desert that the genie ascended and descended? Have you ever considered the rise and fall of your breath? Consider your breath for a moment, it's going on every moment of our lives. Some say life begins with the first inhalation and ends with the last exhale. Do we earn our breath? No, it is a gift. A present that, when paid attention to, may lead you into the Present, the Now, what was, is, and will be.

What a precious gift it is!

Do you have anything more valuable?

No amount of money will buy you more when you run out. Where did this perfect gift come from? Who is the Giver? Follow your breath into the stillness with gratitude to find out. Do you believe in God? Whether you do or don't doesn't matter. I do, but I prefer not to use the term "God"; it carries so many concepts and so much baggage; I like Creator, or Universe, or Infinite one, Elohim; there are many, many other Names for that thing that cannot be named, described, nor held in our thought. The infinite just does not fit in a finite box. When the mind is perfectly still, the heart seems to have the capacity to reflect the infinite and the infinite's love for you and me and all its creation. Do you see how you are so special?

* * *

WE ARE NOT the commentary going on in our heads, that is only a tiny part of who we are, and unless that commentary is directed by the heart, it will never bring fulfillment. A whole universe can only be accessed when the mind has become still, like looking for your reflection in a motionless body of water. It is unclear if the reflection is disturbed by stones, tossed and creating ripples in the water; to see your reflection, the water must be still. Similarly, thoughts create ripples in the water, so how do we tame the mind? Remember the story of the Genie?

I honestly don't know if Prem Rawat is the only source of the techniques of Knowledge or if other paths lead to the same result (Knowledge of Self), I think there might be, but I stopped looking once I found Knowledge. For me, other paths or sources are a distraction from my path.

Why would I follow to see where they lead once I'd been handed the key to the Infinite? The way I've come to love has loved me back beyond my wildest dreams.

I had tried several practices and techniques before I heard about Prem, and maybe if I had stuck with them, they might have taken me to a similar place... or not. You generally stop searching when you find what you've been searching for. Prem himself used to say to search the four corners of the world and if you don't find what you are looking for, then ask, and I can show you that what you are looking for is within you. The cost? Only that you have sincere thirst. Why don't I explain it in detail in this book? First of all, I promised Prem not to reveal the techniques of Knowledge, quality control being one reason for that. If you get 20 people sitting in a circle whispering in the ear of the person four things, how much do you think they'll get corrupted by the 20th person? Now think of thousands, millions. Rather than try to pass that on in my words, I've included a resource chapter at the end of this book where if you want to, you can get the techniques as I did, from a living master.

A little about who Prem Rawat is: He was born in Haridwar, India, in 1957. His father was a Master or Guru with a large following throughout India. Prem used to accompany his father to some of the events his father spoke at. By age four, Prem began addressing the crowds. His message was simple but true "Peace is inside of you" was reported to be the general theme. At eight, Prem's father left the mortal world. It would fall to young Prem to pick up the mantle of his father's work to show seekers of Truth the Knowledge of Self. At age thirteen, Prem accepted an invitation to go to London while on school break. He wasn't in London long when the organizers who had invited him whisked him off to Glastonbury, where they put him onstage as a non-scheduled speaker at the first Glastonbury Festival in 1971. He only spoke a few minutes before the microphone was cut off. Not before many in the audience were moved to receive Knowledge. On the 50th anniversary of that first Glaston-bury Festival, the mayor and council members awarded Prem The Key of Avalon, commemorating his part in the event. Today Prem lives in the US, pilots an airplane, and travels most of the year accepting invitations to speak before huge audiences of up to 500,000 in India to prisons in Africa and Italy, where his Peace Education Program has been adopted to the benefit of both prisoners and prison staff. In India, some prisons have been closed down after implementing PEP because prisoners were no longer returning to prison after release, as had been the case in the past. Prem has also been awarded the title Ambassador of Peace in the EU and South America. He's been honored by the EU, UN, numerous municipalities, and many orga-nizations worldwide. You'll find more about Prem and his lifelong mission to bring peace in the resources chapter.

Exploring inner space and practice of Knowledge occurs mainly through meditation. Some techniques can be experienced 24/7, but sitting down and meditating has the residual benefit of making you centered and giving you a whole new perspective. Starting with an attitude of gratitude. When you begin to recognize all you have to be grateful for, beginning with your breath and the simple fact that you are alive. You have the inner strength, courage, and resources to accomplish anything you focus on. Sitting meditation is the gateway to joy, love, bliss, and clarity that is without bounds. First, you must tame the genie of mind.

Now, the mind is a beautiful thing. We wouldn't be much without it, but it has limitations. It is finite. It is incapable of going where the practice of Knowledge can take us. Mind, if allowed to run wild, can become unruly and difficult to control. The only way I know to still the mind is to give it a glimpse of something so beautiful within that it becomes seduced. Also, practice goes a long way toward taming the mind. A wise man once said whatever you practice, you'll get good at; so true. I'd say it takes both practice and effortless effort. That is your practice when you sincerely love what you're doing. Once you begin to practice Knowledge is hard not to love practicing it. Yet strangely, the mind is adept at finding excuses not to sit and meditate. I guess it doesn't want to relinquish getting all the attention, especially when new to it and there is not much practice history established.

* * *

4
LIVING IN THE NOW

BEING IN THE RIGHT PLACE AT THE RIGHT TIME

When you are rooted in the moment, in now, the present breath, you'll experience many seeming coincidences due to being in the right place at the right time. This is part of the magic I spoke of earlier. Such as thinking of someone, turning a corner, and there they are. Or, like the stories below, all true stories that happened. The first of these occurred in the summer of 1972. A few months after I'd received Knowledge from Prem. I'd been practicing sitting down and meditating for about two hours a day, one in the morning and one before bedtime. There are ways to practice Knowledge as you go through your day, too, and I try to be conscious of it 24/7. I was 18; I'd started college at Goddard College in Plainfield, Vermont, in the Spring and had a month or so before I went back. I decided to take a little trip to Denver and Tucson, where I had addresses for ashrams I wanted to visit. My friend John Spencer wanted to go to California; neither of us had a car, and while hitchhiking had some risks, it was much safer in those days. So we set out from Cleveland - thumbs extended and headed west. We were somewhere in Missouri or Arkansas when we got a ride going all the way to Peru. As tempting as that was, neither of us had passports, so we stuck to our original plans. I remember driving through White Sands, New Mexico, at night with a full blood red moon; it looked like a martian landscape, an impression that might have been enhanced by the joint our host passed around, and also there was the awareness that we were very close to ground zero where the first atom bomb test took place. The sun came up when we were heading west on I-10 through rock formations that looked like a Salvatore Dali landscape.

It was still early when we arrived in Tucson. "Where do you want me to drop you?" Our driver asked. I'd never been to Tucson and had no idea where we were "anywhere along here," I replied. He worked his way over to the curb lane and stopped; I grabbed my backpack and hopped out, wishing John good travels, and we parted ways. I dug around in my backpack for the address of the ashram and started walking. I got maybe a short block before I noticed a house with smiling people on the front porch. I checked the address. I was there! And the smiling people were very welcoming. I wasn't the only guest; it turned out. They came down from Denver/Boulder in a fine white Cadillac convertible, and she was a beauty alright, her face framed by dark curls and a long, lean body - I had a crush. Her name was Jane. She was a few years older than I, probably all of 25. Her traveling companion was an older gentleman; I guessed to be in his 60s, named Harry. Harry owned a shoe store in Boulder and the fine white Cadillac convertible that he drove the 13 yr old Prem around in while he was in Boulder.

I had an aunt and uncle in Santa Fe that I'd planned to visit on my way to Denver. I discovered that Harry and Jane and the fine white Cadillac convertible were going through Santa Fe on their drive back to Denver and would drop me in Santa Fe. So in a few days, we headed north with me in the back seat of the Caddy.

Somewhere near Tuba City, AZ, in the middle of nowhere, a Navaho pickup truck stopped in the road to give a hitchhiker a ride, we stopped, but the car following behind didn't. It came full barrel into the rear of the white Cadillac and slammed us into the pickup.

Now the driver of the Navaho pickup was a tall, big angry Navaho got out of the pickup a walked back toward the white Cadillac with a clenched fist he wanted to plant on whoever rammed his pickup. She got out of the Cadillac, took his fist in her hand, and smiled at him lovingly, saying, " nobody's hurt; it's all okay!!!" ...

He looked at her, confused and disarmed, saying, " somebody better tell me what's goin' on 'cause you're the strangest person I've ever met" She just grinned and swung his arm in hers. Now the car following that had caused the whole mess was driven by a colonel in the US Army who explained a piece of paper fell off his dash, and he bent down to fetch it; looking up again, all he saw was a white Cadillac.

Medicine man Pete Caches - nephew of Black Elk

NOW SHE HAD friends in Tuba City, Doctors who checked us out and put us up for the night while the white Cadillac was made drivable again. The next day we headed toward Santa Fe; when we arrived, I hopped out in front of a Tibetan Buddhist Temple, and the white Caddy with Jane continued to Denver. I went into the temple to get directions to my relatives, and a Buddhist volunteered to give me a ride. So I said thank you very much, and the next thing I was at Aunt Marge & Uncle Robbies. I was welcomed into their home in town and, the next day was taken to see their ranch-let in Galisteo, where they kept a horse I was privileged to ride. Deerskin fringed jacket fringe flew straight out behind me as the horse galloped along, trying its best to dislodge me from its back.

After a few days, I headed up to Denver to 1560 Race Street, where Prem stayed when he was in town. I got one ride out of Santa Fe that took me to Capitol Hill in Denver, the neighborhood I was heading for. There were adventures in Denver working at the Sandoz Wander Co, staying in the ashram, and taking a class in Boulder, but that all gets a little off-topic, so I'll leave that for another time. When I left Denver, I took a bus heading north to the Sioux reservation in Pine Ridge. I had to get across Wyoming, which was notoriously unfriendly to hitchhikers, especially if they looked like a hippie, as I did back then. On the Sioux reservation, I attended a mountain man rendezvous hosted by a medicine man, Pete Catches, the nephew of Black Elk, whose book I'd been reading. Suffice it to say it was a wonderful time, and I felt very present in the moment, living a charmed life.

ANOTHER INSTANCE of being in the right place at the right time was attending an event with Prem speaking to an international audience in Rome's Plaza del' a' Sport. I was waiting for the bus to take me back to my Pensione, and I spotted a beautiful blonde I thought I recognized from Denver. I didn't think I was staring, but we made eye contact, and the next thing I knew, she had her arms around my neck and said, "Hi, my name is Dorothy; what's yours?". We were waiting for the same bus, and it turned out we were staying in the same Pensione. So I invited her to go out for a drink or possibly a bite to eat, and we talked. It got late, and we went back to our Pensione me to my room and her to hers. I woke up the next morning to find her standing beside my bed in a big bathrobe and towel wrapped around her long blond hair. I smiled, greeted her, and invited her to lie down. She accepted by dropping the bathrobe and towel to the floor and lying beside me. She was so soft and smelled so good one thing quickly led to another and, well, you know. I did feel I was living a charmed existence.

These "charmed" moments are always particularly evident when traveling. Traveling often makes me feel like I am taken out of all that is familiar and at the mercy of the Universe. I relinquished control over that which I didn't ever have any control over. Putting myself in the hands of the Universe opened the way to floating along on a river of Grace, to charmed, magical outcomes. It makes it easy to be present.

On the same trip to Rome, I met some folk from Bern, Switzerland, who invited me to come to Bern, so I did. They lived in a small village on Bern's outskirts, easily accessible by train. When I got off the train, I had an address, but I wasn't sure which way to go. So I stopped into the first business I saw to ask for directions which I did in the best German I could muster. My accent gave me away, and the gentleman asked where I was from. His face lit up when he heard I was American; in his youth, he'd played professional Hockey in Canada. He rattled off a few remembrances of Canada and gave me directions. I thanked my new friend and set off again. I'd gone a few blocks only when a car pulled up alongside me, honking. It was my new friend " I think I told you wrong; hop in. I will drive you; it's close ".

YET ANOTHER EXAMPLE of being in the magic was the night I met my wife, Susan.

My roommate was the bass player for Clergy, a punk rock band of the early 80s.

My roommate, Tim West, recommended to me in his Birmingham UK accent that I go to Wallaby's that night because the Kenny Vaughn Band was playing, and they were "really good." Meanwhile, unbeknownst to me, Susan's friend Trixie Merken, bass player for the Kenny Vaughn Band, was twisting her arm to be supportive and go to Wallaby's even though Susan, having just broken up with her boyfriend, was in no mood to go out. Reluctantly she finally agreed. Now Wallaby's wasn't a big club. It was a lovely intimate venue to hear live music. I was sitting in the middle of the room when I remember turning around to see this stunning blonde beauty.

In a yellow and black dress, walk in and through the room to a table near the front. No sooner had she sat down when some guy asked her to dance. She got up and was an exquisite dancer (ballet and modern dance training). She sat down, and I let one song go by to give her a rest before making my way to her table to ask for a dance. She agreed, and I felt like we had such chemistry, the two of us dancing in that room. When the song ended, I walked her back to her table and heard myself suggest to her rather uncharacteristically boldly that I could join her at her table since she was alone. She said she was waiting for friends, and I heard myself reply that I could sit with her until her friends turned up and then get up and go — to which she agreed was reasonable. I was wearing my favorite shirt, which I'd bought in Amsterdam, and a scarf with Sanskrit characters on it I'd bought in Rome. She asked me if I knew what the Sanskrit characters said, and I did my best to interpret them. I must have made a favorable impression because I left Wallaby's with her phone number and a date lined up for the next evening. On my way out, I did meet the friend she'd been waiting for; it was Trixie Merkin.

If the timing had been different.

If I'd not acted uncharacteristically bold.

If I'd not been open to letting the magic happen by being centered in my heart, now.

The next thirty years may have turned out differently. And what an incredible thirty years it was. We were always in love, as only two people in love with life can be. We never argued. We just had a great run of years together.

The practice of Knowledge may not hook you up with a soulmate, but it sure seems to me like if you allow yourself to be in the right place at the right time and follow your heart. The rest will fall into place. Just don't be impatient and chase the wrong thing. You are already complete.

* * *

5

TWO SIDES OF THE SAME COIN

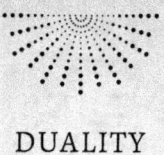

DUALITY

*I*f everything in life is a gift? I mean, it's an interesting premise, right?

If you accept that, then you are accepting every bad thing as well as the good that you've experienced was a gift of life, not a curse of it, so there is gratitude there for lives and deaths as two sides of the same coin. That does not mean grief or loss is not real, not painful. It is more real because you are facing it head-on, and though it may be horrible, it is also sweet when you experience it from a place of inner strength and gratitude. Gratitude for the life that had been.

MY JOB as a web designer and CEO of an international stock photo agency, MyLoupe.com, meant that I spent long hours at a computer. I began to develop what I thought was carpal tunnel syndrome, plus my right hand occasionally would shake almost imperceptibly. My doctor sent me to a neurologist, Dr. Michael Schwartz. It was 2010, I was 56, and Dr. Schwartz said I had Parkinson's Disease. I remember my surprise (is this really happening to me?) And, yes, gratitude that it wasn't worse. I was aware that many people in the world endured worse fates. I was determined not to let it define me. I thanked the doctor and went home with a pile of reading material he'd given me on Parkinson's. What Parkinson's Disease was and was not the current range of treatments, and an appointment to come back in a couple of weeks to discuss treatment. I wasn't looking forward to telling my wife. Susan got home from work and started making dinner. I made the martinis as was our custom and sat down to discuss our days. She asked how my doctor's visit went, so I told her, and without skipping a beat, she said, "That's ok, honey. I'll still love you, and if it ever gets really bad, I'll make you a martini in a sippy cup." With relief, I observed my breath with gratitude. After dinner, I went to my computer and designed a sippy cup martini glass to be sold on cafe press. I'm glad to say I've never needed one and still drink my martinis from a regular martini glass.

SUSAN TOLD the story of when she was a young single mom and got sick, running a high fever and dangerously ill; her doctor had tried to get her to go to the hospital, but she had the little boy at home, no money, she had little to eat so she could feed the boy. She was at home in bed, and the angel of death was in the corner of the room pulling their wings around themself, trying not to be scary and singing sweetly to reassure and calm her that all was ok. But Susan couldn't go with the angel of death then; who'd raise the boy?

Me with Susan around 1983

Susan received the techniques of Self Knowledge in 1984. The first year she had Knowledge, we lived in Denver, Colorado, just off Broadway, in a two-flat. I was getting started working as a photographer then, and when I'd go to the studio in the morning, she'd sit in the bedroom closet and practice Knowledge. I'd come home to find her in a little puddle of bliss. Grinning a huge shit-eating grin, she'd make dinner while I made martinis. She enjoyed life so much.

Fast forward to 2014. I wake up one morning and go downstairs to get my coffee and begin my day, and I find my beloved wife, Susan, lying on the floor. She had just started a new medication for backache, and we thought it could be that. I called the doctor, and he did not think that likely and said I should get her into the emergency room. So I helped her to the car, and off we went to the ER. The doctor looked her over. Her lung capacity seemed good; she was a marathon runner. The doctor was puzzled and had her taken up for a CAT scan.

After she returned to the examination room, we saw the doctor walking by with his lower lip sticking out like a pouting child, and his coffee mug held upside down.

He entered the examination room where we'd been waiting and told us the CAT scan had shown stage four non-smokers lung cancer. It was in her lungs and had spread to her vertebrae and brain, which is why she'd felt like lying down on the floor that morning because of brain swelling. They gave her some meds to reduce the brain swelling and admitted her. It was Feb 12, 2014, thirty-one years and a day since our meeting at Wallaby's. I recall she just said, " This isn't what I had in mind, but I guess this is what we're doing now " I remember hugging her; we both knew she'd been handed a death sentence. I think it was the next day we met with the chief oncologist, who explained that the treatment would be palliative only. We are all on the path to death, and no one can say how long any of us has. She called her boss at Argon National Lab to tell him the news and start her retirement paper-work. She had planned to retire on Dec 31, 2015, but this changed everything. She retired on March 1, 2014, and on May 20, 2014, she exhaled her last breath while I held her hand. As the last breath left her, she smiled as if she were headed into the Light. I believe she is now a part of the universal infinite one that I go to in meditation. Though I knew it was coming, her death devastated me. I knew my roots ran deep, which allowed me to weather the devastation with confidence that even though my life had changed drastically with the loss of my life partner, it was and would continue to be alright. My sister, Betty, came from Tucson to share my grief, and it was so good to have a shoulder to cry on. We went through many, many boxes of Puffs that week.

Prem Rawat was doing a North American tour that Spring / Summer. Susan had wanted to see him, and we'd planned to go to Asheville, North Carolina, to hear him speak in May, But she'd gotten too sick to travel. So she made me promise that if she were gone, I'd go to his remaining events in Toronto and L.A., so I did in late June and July. Seeing Prem in person and hearing him speak is always a treat; my heart always responds. His energy and his words always have a powerful positive effect on me. Through my grief, his words and presence offered further assurance that though it may seem like my world had been ripped apart, it was and would always be alright. I had breath, and I was alive, and what a precious gift that was. Susan had enjoyed that gift too for 64 years, and though she was gone from this life, she was and always would be part of the eternal that can be found within you in stillness, and I could be with her there deep in my heart. My grief gradually turned to gratitude for having had Susan in my life for all those years when I pause to think about that ... what a wonderful gift! Life and Death are two sides of the same coin; as sure as we are born, we will all die. It's a part of life; nothing could be more natural than birth and … death. I now celebrate Susan's life and how it helped shape my own.

I may still get a little choked up; those memories are a bit bittersweet, but I wouldn't trade them for anything. When I lost my beloved wife to cancer, I welcomed the overwhelming emotions of grief that washed over me. They were at once horrible and something to be cherished for honoring the life that was and though death may have claimed the finite being I knew and loved. I have only to look within to find the infinite being within every human being, and she is there too. That is timeless, ageless, universal to us all, and the finite self that has been allowed to recognize and appreciate in gratitude until the end; that is, after all, the nature of 'finite.' Losing Susan did heighten my awareness of my mortality and made me much less of a procrastinator.

"Energy can neither be created nor destroyed."

What is that energy, that life force that departs the body at death?

We often don't like to confront our mortality, but if you don't want to waste the gift of life, get comfortable with the knowledge that it has a limited run. The average lifespan of Seventy-four years is 27,010 days! Eighty-four years 30,660 days. One hundred years is still only 36,500 days. How many of those days are left to you? No one knows, but there is still time to live consciously.

Take a breath ….

Feel the breath fill you with life and exhale as it leaves you to make room for another

Feel the rhythm of your breath as it comes and goes

Know that in this moment, you are alive

The moment that was, is, and will be.

Know the moment of Now

With gratitude, know that

Now is where the magic begins

"Follow the breath within the breath.

Follow the infinite spiral within.

A cycle of breath within another, each in turn going further in.

Without a past or a future, cast in the present.

The eternal now, the expanse of stillness expanding from within each breath.

Everywhere in everything … it leads me on and on again….."

The Chicaguys

6
EXPLORING INNER SPACE WITH KNOWLEDGE

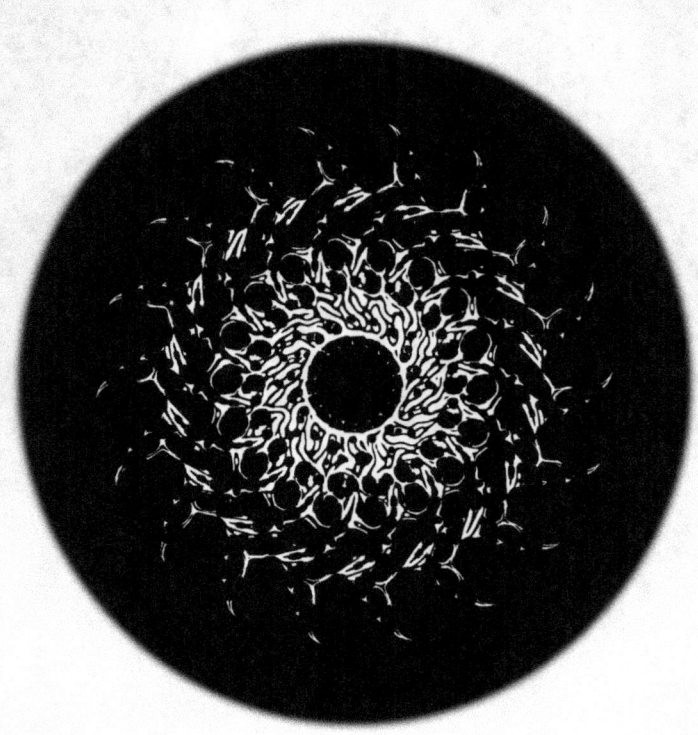

*F*irst, let me explain what I mean and don't mean by inner space. I don't mean exploring your thoughts or the mind. I tried that long ago before I knew any better, and I would not recommend it. It could get downright scary. What I mean is exploring the Heart with the techniques of Knowledge to guide you. When thought stops and your mind is still, you can go deep into Inner Space. How do you get the mind to become still? Practice. If you receive Knowledge from Prem Rawat, you'll be shown how to practice it. And that practice unlocks an inner world of such beauty and power that I am always amazed when I hear someone claim to be bored. I suppose boredom is possible in the outer world but nothing like it in the inner world. One reason I find myself enjoying waiting rooms. No place to go, nothing to do except if you want to close your eyes and take a look inside, it's always beautiful. If you practice any type of meditation, practice it with gratitude.

Exploring inner space and practice of Knowledge occurs mainly through meditation. Some techniques can be experienced 24/7, but sitting down and meditating has the residual benefit of making you centered, and giving you a whole new perspective, starting with an attitude of gratitude. When you begin to recognize all you have to be grateful for, beginning with your breath and the simple fact that you are alive. You have the inner strength, courage, and resources to accomplish anything you focus on. Sitting meditation is the gateway to joy, love, bliss, and clarity that is without bounds. First, you must tame the genie of mind.

Now, mind is a wonderful thing we wouldn't be much without it, but it has limitations. It is finite. It is incapable of going where the practice of Knowledge can take us. Mind, if allowed to run wild, can become unruly and difficult to control. The only way I know to still the mind is to give it a glimpse of something so beautiful within that it becomes seduced. Also, practice goes a long way toward taming the mind. A wise man once said whatever you practice, you'll get good at; so true. I'd say it takes both practice and effortless effort. Effortless effort is the practice you do when you sincerely love what you're doing. Once you begin to practice Knowledge, it is hard not to love practicing it. Yet strangely, the mind is adept at coming up with excuses. I guess it doesn't want to relinquish any control , especially when new to it and there is not much practice history established.

Deep inner space exploration is very thrilling. A few of my experiences in really deep inner space were memorable and transformative. To try to describe them would only be to fall short because there are no words capable of describing the infinite.

Please understand when I write of my experience it is just that, *MY experience*, not a measure of your experience. If you choose to follow this path understand your path is unique to you, your experience is yours alone and should not be judged or measured against someone else's. The same beauty exists in you as in me but our individual experiences of it may vary and evolve as you proceed on the path.

If you practice, you'll get better, and the further into the stillness you go, the easier it gets. I once went into the stillness before bed, and when I emerged, the sun was coming up, and I had but a few hours before I had to go to work. I was not tired at work that day. I can't describe precisely what I experienced except to say I ceased to exist except as the observer. I felt overwhelming love for humanity; I had spent the night with the universal one in a state of infinite consciousness. Just forming those words fills me with peace, even though I know the words can never capture what went on. I can only hold the pale shadow of that experience in my heart, and that fills me. Any human being can know that energy that gives us our breath. The only requirement is that you are alive and thirst to know it.

I don't often go very deep since having had those transformative experiences, maybe because I'm not seeking the really deep inner space experience, and life is already so good, I am very content with my ongoing explorations wherever they take me.

Enlightenment, Samadhi , Nirvana, Satori, Moksha, HaShem, and Heaven all just words but ancient words from different cultures to which we assign deep meaning. Often the same meaning with only subtle differences What is Heaven? According to Wikipedia

" **Heaven** or **the heavens**, is a common religious cosmo-
logical or transcendent supernatural place where beings

such as deities, angels, souls, saints, or venerated ances-
tors are said to originate, be enthroned, or reside.
According to the beliefs of some religions, heavenly
beings can descend to Earth or incarnate and earthly
beings can ascend to Heaven in the afterlife or, in excep-
tional cases, enter Heaven alive. "Wikipedia

This is just my belief as informed by my experience,
that Heaven exists in the Here and Now, not someplace
we may go when we die. Similarly, Hell exists between the
ears of someone lost in fear, anger, and/or confusion.
When I am connected to Now, it sure seems heavenly.

To further explore Wikipedia, this is some of what it
has to say about the term *Nirvana.*

In Indian religions, nirvana is synonymous
with *moksha* and *mukti.*[note 1] All Indian religions assert
it to be a state of perfect quietude, freedom, highest
happiness as well as the liberation from attachment and
worldly suffering and the ending of *samsara,* the round
of existence.[6][7] However, non-Buddhist and Buddhist
traditions describe these terms for liberation differently.
[8] In Hindu philosophy, it is the union of or the realization of the identity of Atman with Brahman, depending
on the Hindu tradition.[9][10][11] In Jainism, nirvana is
also the soteriological goal, representing the release of a
soul from karmic bondage and samsara.[12] In the
Buddhist context, nirvana refers to realization of non-
self and emptiness, marking the end of rebirth by stilling
the fires that keep the process of rebirth going.[8][13]

[14] To achieve this status, one has to get rid of three psychological evils – Raga (greed, desire), Dwesha (anger) and Moha (delusion).

It feels very familiar, " a state of perfect quietude, freedom, highest happiness as well as the liberation from attachment and worldly suffering."
Wikipedia has this to say about Satori:

Satori (悟り) is a Japanese Buddhist term for awakening, "comprehension; understanding".[1] It is derived from the Japanese verb satoru.[2][3]

In the Zen Buddhist tradition, *satori* refers to a deep experience of *kenshō*,[4][5] "seeing into one's true nature". *Ken* means "seeing," *shō* means "nature" or "essence".[4]

Satori and *kenshō* are commonly translated as enlightenment,

You can explore Wikipedia on your own if you feel inclined to do so; my point with these terms is to show this is not new or Eastern or Western but ancient and universal.

* * *

7

LILA AND PERCEPTION

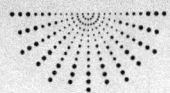

*W*hat is Lila? To quote Wikipedia

" **Lila** (Sanskrit: लीला *līla*) or **leela** (/'liːlə, 'laɪlə/) can be loosely translated as "divine play". The concept of lila is common to both non-dualist and dualist philosophical schools of Indian philosophy, but has a markedly different significance in each. Within non-dualism, lila is a way of describing all reality, including the cosmos, as the outcome of creative play by the divine absolute (Brahman). In the dualistic schools of Vaishnavism, lila refers to the activities of God and his devotee, as well as the macrocosmic actions of the manifest universe, as seen in the Vaishnava scripture *Srimad Bhagavatam*, verse 3.26.4:[1]" Wikipedia

To PERCEIVE Lila as a blessing and Lila "divine play" seems to happen when we are in Now at the right place and time. Remember the stories in chapter 4 on "Living in the Now"? I recall, at the time everything from the rides we got hitchhiking , the white Cadillac, the car crash in the Arizona desert, all of it felt like Lila - the play of the creator with the created. Another more common perception might have been, OMG the white Cadillac was all f***cked up, someone could have been killed, or who the f**ck hit my car. Worry, fear, anger, but all three of us in that Cadillac experienced that event as Lila - a blessing of being played with by the divine, to what end? To teach the very lesson, Being in Now is Being with the divine. I'm getting a bit more theological than I'd intended, but it shows none of this is new. Indeed the scriptures mentioned regarding Lila are around 3000 years old.

The story of Krishna and the Gopis, or cowgirls, illustrates the concept of Lila particularly well. Now Lord Krishna was "God " incarnate, in a more or less human form, maybe looking a little blue, but he was in the Know. The Gopis were young girls who tended cattle for a livelihood and were particularly devoted to Krishna. The. One day they were all in a meadow with their cows, dreaming of Lord Krishna when he manifested himself in fine blue form, one for each of them, and made love to them all in his multiple forms. A classic, if a bit racy, example by judgmental western standards of "divine play" - Lila.

Isn't Lila a point of perception? Isn't Lila a perspective on Life itself?

* * *

8
GRATITUDE

The Mayo Clinic says:
"Expressing gratitude is associated with a host of mental and physical benefits. Studies have shown that feeling thankful can **improve sleep, mood, and immunity**. Gratitude can also **decrease depression, anxiety, difficulties with chronic pain and risk of disease**."

I mentioned an attitude of gratitude earlier, and it will come up again. It bears closer examination. Something very interesting happens when a human being is happy, content, and feeling that peace and appreciation of being alive. Have you ever noticed? They act differently. They become kind. Automatically without being told or without really trying. They are far more likely to let someone with one item jump ahead in the grocery checkout or offer their seat on the bus to someone elderly. Automatically they become kinder, more considerate, and just nicer. If they are feeling empty - not so automatic. When you feel happy and grateful, you feel your humanity. When you are unhappy - not so much.

GRATITUDE IS a choice to recognize the blessings we've been given. If none come to mind, what about the breath you just took? You didn't earn that breath. It was a gift, a present, from who? You are alive, and that miracle is pretty easy to feel grateful for, so experience gratitude and enjoy the experience. Experience your breath with gratitude and enjoy it. In this way, you can let gratitude build on itself.

"When you are touched with admiration, gratitude comes. When you have gratitude, passion comes. When you have passion, compassion comes. When you have compassion, then you have understanding. The cycle continues, and you evolve in this cycle." - Prem Rawat.

"Life is a gift. I want to understand it as clearly as possible before I lose the ability to understand that this life is a gift." - Prem Rawat

Gratitude is fundamental to contentment, serenity, tranquility, peace, joy, love, clarity, and understanding. So much that goes so deep that it is just waiting to be found in every human being.

An old Jewish prayer translated from Hebrew and paraphrased from memory says roughly, "God breathed the breath of life into Adams's nostrils, and Adam returned it as a prayer." That breath is received as a gift, and when we return it as a prayer or meditation with each exhalation, we are indeed blessed—blessed by being in Now, in the moment where life can be lived to the fullest. This, too, evokes gratitude.

* * *

9

STRESS & DISEASE

What is stress, and what causes it? Stress and anxiety are caused by spending too much time worrying about future outcomes you may not have any control over. If there are actions I can take to influence matters favorably, I do them. If out of my control, I try to look at the big picture and understand it will be alright, it already is alright, and it's always been alright. Now, by "alright," I don't mean the way _you_ intended necessarily. You may have to take a universal perspective to see that it's alright.

When I ran MyLoupe stock photo agency, it was just getting to the point of profitability month to month when the great recession of 2007 - 08 hit. Sales were far below monthly overhead, and Microstock was taking a larger and larger share of the market. MyLoupe licensed the publishing rights for images based on the exposure an image would receive. A photo going to be used prominently in a multimillion-dollar ad campaign would cost an order of magnitude more than if the same image were to be used on an internal page of a textbook. One may cost thousands, the other maybe a hundred, if not less. At the same time, Microstock images were licensed for a flat one-dollar licensing fee. A simple by-product of digital cameras getting more affordable and camera phones getting better. Now multimillion-dollar ad campaigns typically hire a photographer over using a stock image unless they found the perfect stock image and could get exclusive rights. So stress is no stranger. I wanted to reduce my stress but felt responsible to the photographers I represented. A solution presented itself when Universal Image Group acquired the MyLoupe collection of those photographers that did not opt-out of their representation.

Anxiety and stress go hand in hand. Anxiety being basically fear. Not necessarily even a rational fear. It isn't always clear with anxiety what is the cause. Trauma suffered in the past is commonly the cause, but rather than spend time looking for the reason I propose to spend that time on the solution - meditation.

If you suffer anxiety recognize your own inner strength to overcome it. You have more strength than you may know. Meditation allows you to access your strength.

Recent studies have shown trees to be far more intelligent than they are given credit for. They communicate with each and care for each other through the vast networks of roots. Trees and fungi form partnerships known as mycorrhizas: Threadlike fungi envelop and fuse with tree roots, helping them extract water and nutrients like phosphorus and nitrogen in exchange for some of the carbon-rich sugars the trees make through photosynthesis. Take a walk in any forest, and you are walking above the subterranean mitochondrial network of fungi and trees. The native people indigenous to Vancouver Island have a saying referring to this that translates to "we are all one." The part of the tree we see above ground is only a part of the whole that includes this subterranean neural net. If you look at trees in a storm, they bend and sway and dance with the storm, but because of their flexibility and roots, they don't get blown over. How can this help you weather an emotional storm or anxiety ? Grow your roots deep with the practice of meditation so when a storm comes, you bend and sway and dance but are not knocked over.

Disease - my doctor, Dr. Ed, once explained disease as dis-ease, the opposite of ease. His prescription - is meditation.

It is well-documented that there are many benefits to meditation. Let us take a look at what it is to meditate.

"to engage in mental exercise (such as concentration on one's breathing or repetition of a mantra) for the purpose of reaching a heightened level of spiritual awareness. transitive verb." - Merriam Webster

To concentrate, but on what? I tried many types of meditation focusing on breathing, zazen, and on a mantra (like Om, or Om mane panda hum) I found the most effective for me to be the techniques of meditation revealed by Prem Rawat as Knowledge. They were passed on to him by his master, who also happened to be his father; they were passed on to him by his master, and so on, living master to living master. Can you learn the same thing in books or from somewhere else? Quite possibly, as I stated earlier, once my thirst had been quenched, I didn't keep searching. I've heard that meditation techniques are documented in some book or another. If I had continued a focused practice of Zen meditation or Kundalini Yoga or Tai Chi, might I have arrived at the same place? Maybe? Those are all good practices, and I have practiced Tai Chi and Hatha Yoga for their physical benefits. But I don't think the value of a living master can be easily disregarded. The inspiration he brings with his humor and words alone I find invaluable. If you should ever get the opportunity to hear him speak live, as with most things live, it's even better than the video. There is something inexplicable that transpires.

"You have the power to overcome the problem. Not the problem overcome you" Prem Rawat.

Don't let your mind wander — Buddha

10

EXPECTATIONS AND CONCEPTS

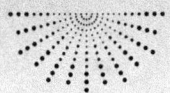

I heard Prem tell a story about answering questions for a room full of people aspiring to receive Knowledge. A woman toward the back of the room raised a hand. She said, " I received knowledge a few weeks ago, and nothing happens; it's not working." The room spun their heads around, expectant of Prem's answer.

Prem asked if she'd been practicing, to which she answered, "Yes." So he told her if it was not working for her, why was she continuing to practice? She should stop.

She countered with, "Oh! No! I love it. It brings me peace and makes me feel so calm and good, but it's not what I thought the Infinite would be like."

This is a case of a concept or expectation getting in the way of the experience. Walk before you run. Your experience will be yours and yours alone. It will possibly differ from your expectation. It may be subtle at first, or it may not.

Expectations and Concepts are both constructs of our minds. Both cloud perception of the Now by existing outside the moment in thoughts past or future. If I am expecting a particular experience might I miss the experience happening now in the present altogether? If it differs from my expectation or even if it meets or exceeds my expectation.

What do you focus on in your life? Do you think this isn't alright? That isn't alright. Why is everything so unjust? Why me? Why do I not have the latest iPhone? Without gratitude, greed comes in. Concepts leave little room for the reality of the matter, particularly if the fact differs from the concept. They can lead to judgments also not based on reality. Free yourself from concepts, and you'll be free to feel that gratitude, to feel this life, to feel and dance with joy in your heart. Free to have that clarity.

It may sound like I am against thinking or critical thought, but I'm not. I only suggest that, instead of thinking about what is missing from our lives, think about the abundance you've been given.

To gain wisdom, the glass must be empty; a full glass has no room. Anything you try to add will spill out. That's why letting go of your concepts is essential. If you want to learn, you must first let go of what you think you already know. I think we all have concepts. Perhaps it is unrealistic to think we can be completely free of all concepts all the time. Maybe a better approach is to apply a large serving of humility over my concepts. In other words, I keep an open mind, for what I think I know is just that, and in a universe of infinite possibilities, who is to say if I really know anything?

When humility leaves, so does wisdom - Prem Rawat.

Happiness has nothing to do with what you have and don't have. Happiness is when you are in touch with yourself" - Prem Rawat.

11

BELIEF VS KNOWING

I just finished the last chapter with "who is to say if I know anything at all," so what's with this knowing? The only thing I am really confident of is experiential Knowing. That which rings true with the heart, other things that I "know" I try to keep an open mind on. Consider Pluto; when I was young, it was a planet in our solar system; now - not so much. Love cannot be scientifically proven when you are in Love - you Know. Some things I think I know, like "the ninth planet of our solar system is Pluto," may not be correct. Keeping an open mind might be better than being intractable in what you know.

If I tell you the afternoon sun is warm, you can experience the sun's warmth on your skin, feel it, and see the sun's brightness in the sky. These are attributes of the sun you can know. No belief or faith is required because we can experience the sun. If I say there are billions of stars in the universe, many are suns brighter than our own. That might require a belief or faith in the science of astronomy. I can see many stars in the night sky if I'm not in a brightly lit city, but billions. I can't even conceive of a billion. And brighter than our sun? Unless you are an astronomer conducting research, you probably have to accept or not accept that on faith. Faith in science requires belief in many things you cannot experience. We take many simple truths for granted that we know by our experience of them - water is wet, fire is hot. If you are walking on a hot sandy beach, you know the sand is hot on your bare feet. There are also many things we accept on faith. Whether science or religion, both ask us to believe and have faith in things that others are experts whom we have entrusted with interpreting these mysteries for us. That may be alright for some topics but not for Knowledge of the Self. That is a topic that you alone are uniquely qualified for.

I once hear Prem say, "if you are waiting for an angel to come down and save you, I have news. That angel is here; no, it's not me; it's you. You are that angel. You are the only one qualified to save you. Not saying you're qualified to save anyone else, but you are uniquely qualified to save yourself ".

. . .

THE TWO WOLVES is a story I've heard Prem tell that makes an important point. Once upon a time, there was a village and a chief. One day a young boy went to question the chief. He asked, "Chief, I am confused; how is it that some people who seem good do some bad things?" The chief said, " Everyone has two wolves inside them, a good wolf and a bad wolf, that are fighting each other for control. Sometime one might be in control; sometimes it's the other". The boy asked, "Which wolf wins?" The chief answered, "the one who is fed." Which wolf do you feed?

* * *

12

CREATIVITY

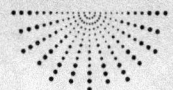

I don't know if this is true for everyone, but I believe everyone has creative ability. It may be buried, but I think it is there, more developed and nurtured in some. But it has to be developed and nurtured in anyone. I have been blessed to have earned my living in the creative world most of my life; my first foray into this creative world was deciding to make a living as a photographer. A profession that afforded me the opportunity for creative expression and sometimes hanging out with some fascinating people from U.S. Senator Edward "Ted" Kennedy to Chicago Blues legends Koko Taylor and Sunnyland Slim. I was a working photographer for about ten years when I took computer graphics classes at the Art Institute of Chicago, and I learned about a new thing called the World Wide Web. I began teaching myself HTML, the markup language of the World Wide Web, and when Montgomery Wards closed down, business for freelance photographers in Chicago suddenly got tougher. As a photographer, I built a website for myself and showed some of my early experimental Photoshop work, my "foto-art." I was among the first hundred or so photographers to pioneer the World Wide Web. That caught the eye of some zines—Photon *Magazine* out of the UK and *Shutterbug* in the US. As the work for photographers in Chicago got scarcer, I found myself at a temp agency hawking my recently developed World Wide Web skills. I was soon hired at a new Web startup, Digital Interface. It wasn't long before they made me an offer to hire me permanently. I accepted and soon made more money than I ever had to do something I loved.

Digital interface, like so many other dot com startups, did not survive the dot com bust . I ended up agreeing to take over a few of their clients and starting on my own, finding a PHP programmer in Kolkata, India, to work with me in combining a passion for photography with a passion for technology; together, we built MyLoupe.com, the stock photographer's marketplace. The concept was a stock photo website where photographers did some of the work of uploading and keywording, then earned 75-90% of each sale compared to 30% or less from most stock houses. Unfortunately, that only worked for a few that took full advantage of the programs offered. I, at one point, had the privilege of representing over 1000 talented photographers worldwide. MyLoupe ended after the great recession of 2007- 08; in 2013, 3 years after my Parkinson's diagnosis, MyLoupe.com was acquired by Universal Image Group. That relieved a lot of stress.

I continued with my own personal artwork. I was taking photos that felt like they captured a beautiful moment and then applying various algorithms to abstract the image in varying degrees to evoke a feeling that could sometimes engage the viewer more by requiring a little more imagination. The illustrations in this book are an example of some black-and-white styles I've had fun with. If you'd like to see more, take a visit to https://brian heston.net.

I've sold a few pieces here and there. The local annual Beverly Artwalk here in Chicago, the Fusion Gallery in Palm Springs, and the Calavera Gallery in Italy. But I was grateful I didn't need to earn a living from it.

You can't help but create when you look at your surroundings with eyes of love. Again it is perspective and perception and a connection to the heart, that place of love, peace, beauty, and clarity that exists within every human being, that gives you the perception of "eyes of love." Seeing that beauty that verges on overwhelming in everyday things around me, a shadow, a reflection, a caress of sunlight, inspired me to become a photographer and an artist. To capture a slice of time in an image still can boggle my mind if I think about it. *Eyes of Love* is the title of a song I wrote and recorded as The Chicaguys.

Music is another realm that attracts me to be creative. Ears of love? Maybe more like the heart of love because music can get straight to the core. I've had a passion for music most of my life. I frequently go out to see live music, from opera to rock and roll. About 2017, I became a student of music. Parkinson's and the tremor in my hand were the excuses that held me back most recently, but on December 31, 2016, I underwent a surgical procedure known as Deep Brain Stimulation. The result... no more tremor, no more excuse, so my present to myself after I recovered from the surgery was a shiny new red Fender Stratocaster - electric guitar, which I have become a student of music and learning to play.

I also delved into home recording studio production and synthesizer and have released three albums and a few singles to date as The Chicaguys (theChicaguys.com). They are distributed through Distro Kid and can be found on most streaming platforms (Spotify, Amazon, Apple Music, iTunes, Tidal, Napster, Deezer, and others). If you want to hear a sample, here's one of my favorites on https://www.youtube.com/watch?v=i8tD7W8aPNc

YouTube video of "Shifting Sands" by the Chicaguys

THE MOTIVATION for releasing music was firstly so I could listen to it with my girlfriend and because I felt I had something to say, and what better way to share a feeling?

So my point in writing about my creativity is only to suggest that it comes from the same place within, and once you begin to tap into that place, I think you'll find the key to your own creativity. That's my belief, anyway.

As someone who received Knowledge and practiced it, I can say it has exceeded anything I hoped it would be. It has been transformative, and my life has been magical. What do I mean by magical? I followed my heart on many different things that worked out almost too good to be true.

Deciding to pursue photography as a career. Deciding to pursue music (the Chicaguys have reached over 36,000 listeners on Spotify alone in about 18 months since 2021!).

You may find a new wellspring of creativity if you are already creative. When you have a feeling inside that you can't contain, that is when you must make music, make art, and write books. That is when you dance with the joy you find within.

"There is always something happening that is very joyful inside of you... Stop what you're doing and feel the joy of that breath" - Prem Rawat.

* * *

13

MAGICAL LIFE

Today I do live a magical life. I live in an exciting major US city, Chicago, I am only 20 minutes from the heart of the city, full of activities and culture to be enjoyed. I live on the edge of a forest preserve in one of the quietest neighborhoods in the city. I have a 1922 Chicago Bungalow, which has been renovated into my dream home and studio. It is a beautiful home.

My neighbors are all lovely, and directly across the street is where my beautiful girlfriend lives. I spend the worst of the winter months with my girlfriend, enjoying the desert climate of Palm Springs, California. In my spare time, when I am not writing, practicing guitar, or playing with art, I am composing, playing, and recording music or writing. How much fun is that? I have such gratitude for everything in my life, but particularly for my breath, without which I'd not have a life. Twelve years with Parkinson's, and it barely affects me at all; I enjoy long walks in the forest and this beautiful neighborhood.

I do live a life filled with Gratitude. I have everything I could want in this world, and in the realm *not* of this world, I am filled with Contentment, Peace, Fulfillment, and Joy; each breath brings new Joy. This has to be Heaven Here, Now. Join me. Won't you?

the Author

Dance to the rhythm of life

14

RESOURCES

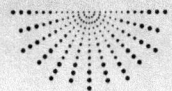

For anyone wanting to learn more about transforming your life into a magical one where you live in the land of Now and enjoy inner peace, love, joy, and clarity, here are the promised resources to take you on your way. There is a mobile app called Timeless Today, and you can download or visit the website at https://www.timelesstoday.tv/peak-is-here. Once you open the app, search for PEAK (Peace Education And Knowledge). PEAK is a series of videos Prem has put together to answer any questions or doubts and an interactive section for reflecting on what is covered in the videos. All leading to receiving this Knowledge I have spoken of if you choose to ask for it. If you choose this path, remember practice is required to reap the benefits.

Following my heart into other creative endeavors has been so much fun. I get to have so much fun almost all the time; it hardly seems fair if you're not. It is a simple matter of choice. Choosing to know your true self that resides within your heart reflects the infinite that is, was, and will be. The life force energy has no beginning or end. There are no words that can fully express my gratitude for this Knowledge. My heart is overflowing with that gratitude, and that makes everything magical. If you take anything away from this book, I hope it is a thirst to know within yourself what I've tried to describe. Find your peace. In several parts of this book, I have expressed my experience of personal peace. The important takeaway is not my experience of peace but yours.

IF YOU HAVE a thirst for more, explore the links below. May your journey and your magical story begin.

Prem Rawat. (n.d.). *PEAK: Know Yourself.* https://www. premrawat.com/peak-know-yourself

Rawat, P. (2021, July 5). *Chapter 1: Introduction.* Prem Rawat. https://www.premrawat.com/peak-know-your

self/54-watch-introductions-to-the-peak-chapters/3-chapter-1-peak-introduction

TimelessToday. (n.d.). https://www.timelesstoday.tv/peak-is-here

Apple Mobile Apps. (n.d.). Apple Mobile Apps. https://Mobile App (Apple) https://apps.apple.com/us/app/timelesstoday/id1296216379

TimelessToday - Apps on Google Play. (n.d.). https://play.google.com/store/apps/details?id=com.app.timelesstoday

Words of Peace Global is an independent charitable foundation set up by individuals inspired by Global Ambassador of Peace and Author Prem Rawat's powerful and unique message. *Words of Peace*. (2022). https://www.wopg.org

YouTube Channel https://www.youtube.com/premrawatofficial

Watch and Listen Library https://www.premrawat.com/watch-listen-read/practical-peace-library#

Highly recommended Prem's NY Times Best Seller *HEAR YOURSELF How to Find Peace in a Noisy World* https://www.premrawat.com/hear-yourself-book

The Prem Rawat Foundation TPRF advances **dignity**, **peace**, and **prosperity** by addressing fundamental human needs. https://tprf.org/

More on the intelligence of trees https://www.intelligent-trees.com/

* * *

15

CONCLUSION

I have one responsibility in this life above any other. My responsibility is to ensure I am at peace now, in contentment, clarity, and love. Having fun, real fun. I'm talking about the kind of fun you can have hanging out with the Divine, now that's some serious fun. If everyone took that responsibility seriously, there would be world peace.

"All know the drop merges with the ocean; few understand the ocean also merges with the drop" - Kabir.

Realize that you are the drop and each drop contains the ocean at its core, but that its existence as a drop is very brief, if it does not recognize the ocean it contains it will miss the opportunity of its existence which may not come again. Or it can recognize the ocean and realize the purpose of its brief existence, and enjoy the magnificence of the infinite ocean of the Divine.

It has occurred to me that others have lived fifty years or so with this Knowledge, and I wondered what stories they might have. I've invited several to share their stories and publish them here at Ocean in the Drop Publishing. So if you've enjoyed this book and would like to read other life stories of magic, send your email to oceandrop pub@gmail.com. I'll add it to our list, and you'll be notified whenever a new book comes out. Also, if you have questions or comments you wish to address to me, you can use the publisher's email above. Please if you've enjoyed this book, leave a review. If you have a thirst for more, explore the links in Chapter 14. May your journey and your magical story begin. Maybe it already has.…

* * *